Welcome To
I Spy everything

GOOD LUCK

I Spy With My Little eye Something Beginning with

a Is For
Airplane

I Spy With My Little eye Something Beginning with...

b Is For

Bicycle

I Spy With My Little eye
Something Beginning with...

C Is For

Catapillar

I Spy With My Little eye Something Beginning with...

d Is For

daisy

I Spy With My Little eye Something Beginning with...

e Is For

elephant

I Spy With My Little eye Something Beginning with...

 Is For

frog

I Spy With My Little eye Something Beginning with...

g Is For

gold

I Spy With My Little eye Something Beginning with...

h Is For

holly

I Spy With My Little eye Something Beginning with...

i Is For

ice cream

I Spy With My Little eye Something Beginning with...

j Is For

Jaguar

I Spy With My Little eye Something Beginning with...

k Is For

king

I Spy With My Little eye Something Beginning with...

Is For

ladybug

I Spy With My Little eye
Something Beginning with...

m Is For

moon

I Spy With My Little eye Something Beginning with...

N Is For 123

Numbers

I Spy With My Little eye Something Beginning with...

O Is For

owl

I Spy With My Little eye
Something Beginning with...

P Is For

pear

I Spy With My Little eye Something Beginning with...

q Is For

Quack`

I Spy With My Little eye
Something Beginning with...

r Is For

rainbow

I Spy With My Little eye Something Beginning with...

 **Is For**

Snake

I Spy With My Little eye Something Beginning with...

Is For

Turtle

I Spy With My Little eye
Something Beginning with...

U Is For

Umbrella

I Spy With My Little eye Something Beginning with...

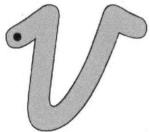 Is For

vet

I Spy With My Little eye Something Beginning with...

W Is For

walrus

I Spy With My Little eye
Something Beginning with...

X Is For xylophone

I Spy With My Little eye Something Beginning with...

Y Is For

Yellow

I Spy With My Little eye Something Beginning with...

Z Is For

zebra

Printed in the USA
CPSIA information can be obtained
at www.ICGtesting.com
LVHW082318031224
798267LV00045B/1952